GUILT
Living Guilt Free

JUNE HUNT

ROSE PUBLISHING/ASPIRE PRESS

Carson, California

ROSE PUBLISHING/ASPIRE PRESS

Guilt: Living Guilt Free
Copyright © 2013 Hope For The Heart
All rights reserved.
Aspire Press, a division of Rose Publishing, Inc.
17909 Adria Maru Lane
Carson, California 90746 USA
www.aspirepress.com

Register your book at www.aspirepress.com/register
Get inspiration via email, sign up at www.aspirepress.com

All Scripture quotations, unless otherwise indicated, are
taken from the Holy Bible, New International Version®
NIV®. Copyright © 1973, 1978, 1984, 2011 by Biblica, Inc.™
Used by permission. All rights reserved worldwide.

Scripture quotations marked "NKJV" are taken from the
New King James Version. Copyright © 1982 by Thomas
Nelson, Inc. Used by permission. All rights reserved.

Scripture quotations marked "ESV" are taken from
The Holy Bible, English Standard Version. Copyright ©
2000; 2001 by Crossway Bibles, a division of Good News
Publishers. Used by permission. All rights reserved.

Printed by Regent Publishing Services Ltd.
Printed in China
November 2015, 3rd printing

CONTENTS

ear friend,

"The thrill of victory—the agony of defeat."
In North America, this saying dominated the sports world for many years. Yet on a personal level, I know what it's like to experience both extremes.

Never will I forget the crisp, fall evening when a dear friend and I attended a Dallas Cowboys football game. Coach Tom Landry executed the game plan perfectly. Quarterback Roger Staubach was never better. This night truly epitomized the thrill of victory.

Instead of scurrying away with all the fans and fighting the traffic, Barbara and I decided to stay in our seats and simply talk. As we watched Texas Stadium empty, we saw 65,000-plus vacant blue stadium seats in bright contrast to the brilliant green AstroTurf. But as Barbara and I continued to talk, instead of maintaining that thrill of victory, I began to feel the agony of defeat. My mind became crowded with guilt because of my own wrong choices in the past.

I remember saying to Barbara, "I don't deserve to have you as my grace friend." (She always gave me grace when I didn't deserve it.) And then I began a litany of wrong choices that I had made over the years. Tears filled my eyes as I thought about certain people whom I had hurt—people including Barbara.

"How could I have done that?" I lamented. "How could I have thought that way!"

After I had poured out my heart, Barbara took my hand and said something that stunned me. "June, I don't think you really understand what grace is all about."

What? I thought. *I understand grace. I've even taught others about grace.*

Then Barbara reiterated, "I don't think you understand the grace of God for you."

Could this be true? Could I know grace in my head, but not in my heart?

Barbara continued, "June, you apply grace to others, but not to yourself." To be candid, I had no clue that this was true.

Ultimately, she shared truth that I knew was accurate, but truth that I wasn't appropriating in my heart. She reminded me:

"We've all been guilty of breaking God's law. June, you are no different" (Romans 3:23).

"Since you confessed your sins and have given your life to Christ, God was faithful to forgive your sins and cleanse you from all unrighteousness" (1 John 1:9). "You've already received God's gift of grace—giving you the forgiveness you didn't deserve" (Ephesians 2:8–9). "Jesus forgave all your sins—past, present, and future—so that you could be saved and live guilt-free" (Hebrews 10:10).

I knew Barbara had spoken the truth, and there's nothing like truth to set us all free. What relief. What a load off my shoulders!

Unquestionably, Barbara was right. I hadn't applied grace to my own life. I needed God's grace like a blanket over my heart so that I wouldn't live with the coldness of false guilt.

If that's your need, may I encourage you to embrace God's heart on living guilt free. Being free of guilt has everything to do with grace. There's a very good reason why grace is called "amazing."

Yours in the Lord's hope,

June Hunt

GUILT
Living Guilt Free

Two men experience an immense amount of guilt and their lives are changed forever. One man's guilt leads to repentance, allowing him to live guilt free the rest of his life. The other man's guilt leads to gut-wrenching grief, compelling him to take his own life.

Though tethered together by bad decisions, the two couldn't be more different. One we call David—but God calls him,*"a man after my own heart ... "* (Acts 13:22). The other we call Judas—but Jesus knew him as the one *"who would betray him"* (John 6:64).

Obviously, God uses guilt to get our attention, but He never designed guilt to distress us forever. God created guilt to prick a calloused conscience, to move us to repent, to convict us of our wrong, and to convince us to do right.

The Bible gives this assurance: When we *"confess our sins"* with complete humility, God purifies our heart and forgives our every sin.

"If we confess our sins, he is faithful and just and will forgive us our sins and purify us from all unrighteousness."
(1 John 1:9)

DEFINITIONS

"Judas, are you betraying the Son of Man with a kiss?" (Luke 22:48).

The question should send shock waves through his conscience, stopping him dead in his tracks, challenging him to change his diabolical plan. Betraying a friend is two-faced, but to do so with a kiss is nothing less than cruel.

Meanwhile, the jealous religious leaders can't wait to rid themselves of Jesus. After all, the crowds keep coming to Him—the One with purest motives—but His truth-filled teachings keep shining a spotlight on their own spiritual darkness.

So for 30 pieces of silver, Judas agrees to deliver Jesus into the leaders' murderous hands. Perceptively, Jesus speaks boldly about His betrayer and the guilt that will beset him.

> **"Woe to that man who betrays the Son of Man! It would be better for him if he had not been born."**
> **(Matthew 26:24)**

One day, true guilt grabs hold of Judas. Yet his consuming sense of regret becomes a roadblock to repentance and life change. That's not God's game plan for guilt.

As a member of Jesus' inner circle of 12 original disciples, being a betrayer seems inconceivable. After all, Judas was there when Jesus calmed the storm and walked on water. Judas was there when Jesus multiplied a few fish and bites of bread to feed over 5,000. Judas was there when Jesus drove out demons, healed the sick, and raised the dead.

How could he not believe! And yet, Jesus directs the following statement straight at Judas, *"There are some of you who do not believe"* (John 6:64).

Talk of heaven and eternity and total forgiveness of sins—these intangibles are far too trivial. And with Jesus now talking about His impending death, disillusioned Judas focuses on the material world— and resorts to monetary gain for his devious betrayal. So just how do the religious leaders perceive this mercenary plot? *"They were delighted and agreed to give him money"* (Luke 22:5).

▶ **True guilt** is the fact of being at fault or committing an offense.[1]

▶ **True guilt** is the result of any wrong attitude or action that is contrary to the perfect will of God.

▶ **"True guilt"** in Hebrew is *asham*, which paints a three-dimensional picture: doing wrong, deserving punishment, and demanding a penalty so that fellowship with God can be restored.²

After David committed adultery with Bathsheba, he confessed and repented, and from a contrite heart cried out to God:

"Against you, you only, have I sinned and done what is evil in your sight." (Psalm 51:4)

David realized that any and all sinful actions are first and foremost against God, for it is God who declared adultery to be against His moral law and in opposition to His character: *"You shall not commit adultery"* (Exodus 20:14).

Responding to True Guilt

QUESTION: **"What should I do when I know I'm guilty and hate feeling guilty?"**

ANSWER: You experience true guilt when you recognize the fact that you have sinned.

Upon gaining that knowledge, the Bible says you are to *"confess"* to God ("agree" with God) that you have sinned and have fallen short of being right in God's sight. If you have entered into a personal, saving relationship with God through accepting the death of Jesus Christ as payment for your sins and receiving Him into your life as your Savior and Lord, then you are a child of God and can rightfully claim the forgiveness of Christ. But like David, you must approach God with a humble and contrite heart, a heart broken over your sin against God.

- ▶ **Note the honesty of David**: *"I acknowledged my sin to you and did not cover up my iniquity"* (Psalm 32:5).

- ▶ **Reflect on God's response to David**: *"And you forgave the guilt of my sin"* (Psalm 32:5).

- ▶ **Know what God says about you**: *"I will forgive their wickedness and will remember their sins no more"* (Jeremiah 31:34).

God is faithful. He will always do what He says He will do. Just as He extended forgiveness to David, His response is the same to you. Not only has God forgiven you, He has also removed your sins from you.

WHAT IS False Guilt?

Does Simon Iscariot know about his son's deception and duplicity? Does the earthly father of the world's most infamous traitor experience false guilt from Judas' being a false friend—the conspiring "friend" of Christ?

As Simon watches Judas as a young boy skip along dusty paths, does he—as most dads—muse about what kind of man his son might become? Does he try to groom Judas to be a model citizen who contributes much to his community? Now—if he's aware of Judas' unconscionable conspiracy—is he wracked with false guilt, somehow blaming himself for his son's failure, writhing in shame over a son who sells out his close friend?

Since personal responsibility is a frequent theme in the Bible and since Judas is an adult, his father bears no blame for the betrayal of the Savior. Ezekiel 18:20 clearly makes this point:

> "The child will not share the guilt of the parent, nor will the parent share the guilt of the child."

From time to time, we've all fallen prey to false guilt—especially if someone in our lives is skilled at *guilt-manipulation*—a powerful method of control. God designed guilt to convict us of our sin, to convince us to change, to cause us to accept Christ—for Him to cleanse us and develop His character in us. However, guilt-manipulators use false guilt to try to direct us in such a way that we develop *people-pleasing* characteristics.

▶ God uses "good" or true guilt so that we will gain freedom from sin's power in our lives.

▶ Guilt-manipulators use false guilt so that we will stay fearful, and they will gain power over our lives.

Simply put, guilt-manipulators want to control us—they need people pleasers who are desperate for their approval. Notice how the apostle Paul refused to fall into this trap:

> " ... we speak as those approved by God to be entrusted with the gospel.
> We are not trying to please people but God, who tests our hearts."
> (1 Thessalonians 2:4)

- ▶ **False guilt** is based on self-condemning feelings that you have not lived up to your own expectations or those of someone else.[3]

- ▶ **False guilt** arises when you blame yourself even though you've committed no wrong or after having done something wrong, you've confessed and turned from your sin.

- ▶ **False guilt** keeps you in bondage to three destructive masters: shame, fear, and anger.

- ▶ **False guilt**, ironically, is not resolved by confession because, as a factual matter, there is nothing to confess. Confession won't be effective because false guilt is not based on truth but rather a lie.

Realize, if you continually feel guilty or condemned, the source could be Satan. Revelation 12:10 says that Satan is the *"accuser of our brothers and sisters, who accuses them before our God day and night."* He loves to disseminate lies, to burden true believers with false guilt and feelings of eternal condemnation. Some of his favorite strategies include: bringing up the past, reminding you of your failures, and making you feel unforgiven by God and unaccepted by God. Jesus explains one of the core tactics of the enemy:

**"He was a murderer from the beginning,
not holding to the truth,
for there is no truth in him.
When he lies, he speaks his native language,
for he is a liar and the father of lies."
(John 8:44)**

Responding to False Guilt

QUESTION: "I've been told I struggle with false guilt. What can I do when I can't stop thinking about sins I've confessed and that I no longer do?"

ANSWER: The next time the viewing screen of your mind begins to replay your repented sins—sins you have confessed that have been forgiven and you are no longer committing—realize this taunting comes from Satan, the accuser, to discourage you. Ask yourself:

▶ "What am I hearing?" (False Accusation.)

▶ "What am I feeling?" (False Guilt.)

▶ "What are the facts?" (I am no longer guilty because I have been fully forgiven.)

Use Scripture as your standard to determine true and false guilt. If you have received Jesus Christ as your personal Lord and Savior, He took away your sins when He died. Rather than focusing on false accusations and false guilt, choose to focus on God's truth.

Turn Romans 8:1 into a prayer: "Thank You, Father, that You don't condemn me and don't want me to condemn myself. These feelings of false guilt are not valid because I've accepted Christ as my Lord and Savior and have turned away from my sin."

> "There is now no condemnation
> for those who are in Christ Jesus."
> (Romans 8:1)

It's the very night of the betrayal. Jesus and His 12 disciples have gathered to celebrate the Passover. The conversation suddenly takes a sobering turn when Jesus flatly states, *"Truly I tell you, one of you will betray me"* (Matthew 26:21).

The disciples—11 of them, that is—become deeply disturbed and begin asking one by one, *"Surely you don't mean me, Lord?"* And then Judas, knowing full well his two-faced intentions, inquires, *"Surely you don't mean me, Rabbi?"* Jesus speaks truth, *"You have said so."* Then Judas slithers off to commit his despicable deed (Matthew 26:22–25).

Yet there has been one detectable clue as to the identity of this traitor—even before Jesus points out Judas. Judas addresses Jesus as *"Rabbi"* which means "Teacher," but never as "Lord." Why the distinction? Judas hasn't allowed Jesus to be Lord of his life; he hasn't yielded his rights to the Lord's rule; he hasn't submitted himself to Christ's sovereignty. In truth, Judas is unrepentant and unsaved, still a slave to sin, still held captive in the grip of guilt.

> **"As soon as Judas took the bread,**
> **Satan entered into him.**
> **So Jesus told him,**
> **'What you are about to do, do quickly.'"**
> **(John 13:27)**

Judas experienced true guilt because he was truly guilty. However, it's not uncommon to feel guilty even when we're not guilty. When we think something is wrong that isn't or when someone we trust tells us we've done something wrong that we haven't, we can receive those thoughts as truth when they're actually a lie.

The Contrast

Consider these two kinds of guilt: One is a friend who speaks truth, gently leading you to repentance and forgiveness. The other is a secret conspirator who taunts and condemns, bringing dishonor and inner shame.[4] The Bible gives this warning:

> **"Be alert and of sober mind.
> Your enemy the devil prowls around like a
> roaring lion looking for someone to devour."
> (1 Peter 5:8)**

▶ **True Guilt** *"When he, the Spirit of truth, comes, he will guide you into all truth"* (John 16:13).

▶ **False Guilt** *"For the accuser of our brothers and sisters [Satan], who accuses them before our God day and night, has been hurled down"* (Revelation 12:10).

▶ **True Guilt is** based on fact.

- "I realize I was wrong to take certain office supplies home for my personal use. I have to admit this is actually stealing."

▶ **False Guilt** is based on feelings.

- "I sure could use those office supplies at home. I feel horrible. I'm horrible for wanting something that isn't mine."

"If anyone, then, knows the good they ought to do and doesn't do it, it is sin for them" (James 4:17).

▶ **True Guilt** results in a godly sorrow over sin.

- "My failure to be honest makes me aware of how much I don't reflect the character of Christ. I'm truly sorry and sincerely want to change. That's my commitment."

▶ **False Guilt** results in a worldly sorrow over consequences.

- "I have confessed that I was dishonest, but I feel so condemned by those around me. "

"Godly sorrow brings repentance that leads to salvation and leaves no regret, but worldly sorrow brings death. See what this godly sorrow has produced in you: what earnestness, what eagerness to clear yourselves, what indignation, what alarm, what longing, what concern, what readiness to see justice done. At every point you have proved yourselves to be innocent in this matter" (2 Corinthians 7:10–11).

▶ **True Guilt** brings conviction.

- "I now see that holding on to my anger toward him isn't a solution. I need to confront the situation and admit where I've been wrong."

▶ **False Guilt** brings condemnation.

- "I have confessed my sin regarding anger. I know God hates the evil that was done. I feel like He hates me for my feelings."

"There is a time for everything ... a time to love and a time to hate, a time for war and a time for peace" (Ecclesiastes 3:1, 8).

▶ **True Guilt** results in repentance.

- "I truly want to be a person of integrity. I promise I'll make restitution and pray for the Lord's strength to change this bad habit. I'm genuinely sorry that I was dishonest."

▶ **False Guilt** results in retreating.

- "I have made restitution and prayed that God would forgive me, but I feel it's hopeless—I can't change."

"I will give you a new heart and put a new spirit in you; I will remove from you your heart of stone and give you a heart of flesh. And I will put my Spirit in you and move you to follow my decrees and be careful to keep my laws" (Ezekiel 36:26–27).

▶ **True Guilt** accepts forgiveness.

- "I am thankful that I have a heavenly Father who will always forgive me, no matter what I have done."

▶ **False Guilt** attempts to earn forgiveness.

- "I've asked God to forgive me, but I can't do enough to feel forgiven."

"All the prophets testify about him that everyone who believes in him receives forgiveness of sins through his name" (Acts 10:43).

▶ **True Guilt** focuses on Christ's works.

  ▪ "Only by relying on Jesus Christ to meet my needs and on His redeeming work within me will I be able to be the person I was created to be. Because of His gift of grace, it's my joy to do whatever work God has for me."

▶ **False Guilt** focuses on personal good works.

  ▪ "The more good works I do the better I feel. I'm driven to do everything well so that the good will outweigh the bad. I'm afraid if I don't do enough, I'll be rejected."

"For it is by grace you have been saved, through faith—and this is not from yourselves, it is the gift of God—not by works, so that no one can boast" (Ephesians 2:8–9).

▶ **True Guilt** brings reconciliation with God and others.

  ▪ "I know God loves me unconditionally, which motivates me to be more loving and forgiving of others."

▶ **False Guilt** brings rejection from God and others.

  ▪ "God could never love me. If others get close enough to see what I am really like, they'll reject me too."

"I have loved you with an everlasting love; I have drawn you with unfailing kindness" (Jeremiah 31:3).

In a nutshell, *true guilt* shows us where we have erred and where we need to change. It is the appropriate response and what we should feel when we have truly sinned. It motivates, pushes, and prods us to be all that God created us to be. It is healthy and helpful.

By contrast, *false guilt* reminds us of our shortcomings and undermines our spiritual growth. It leads to disappointment, discouragement, depression, and despair. It immobilizes us when we should be moving forward. It hinders our development, stunts our growth, and restricts our freedom. It weighs us down and keeps us from becoming the people God wants us to be. Knowing the difference between true guilt and false guilt is critical for those who want to walk in freedom.

"Then you will know the truth, and the truth will set you free." (John 8:32)

Feeling Happy When Sinning

QUESTION: "If I am supposed to feel guilty when I sin, why do I sometimes feel happy when I am sinning?"

ANSWER: Scripture does not say that sin is unpleasant. Quite the contrary! Sin would not be a problem if it was unpleasant and held no appeal. The lure to sin is based on the fact that it feels good to our flesh and results in feelings of temporary happiness because some of our fleshly desires have been satisfied—temporarily. But the Bible warns that sinful pleasure is brief—a pleasure that lasts but a moment when compared to eternity.

"The mirth of the wicked is brief, the joy of the godless lasts but a moment." (Job 20:5)

Shame sends Judas into a death spiral. To him, there is no way to right a horrible wrong. With his emotions reeling, the wretched betrayal of Jesus dooms his life—forever.

The hope of forgiveness never enters his mind, so shame sends disgrace upon his soul. The agony of shame is poured out in the Psalms.

> **"I live in disgrace all day long,**
> **and my face is covered with shame."**
> **(Psalm 44:15)**

Most people assume that *guilt* and *shame* are basically the same. However, guilt focuses on *what we've done* while shame focuses on *who we are*.

The goal of guilt is to convict us of committing a wrongful act so that we will confess it, be forgiven for it, then change it. The outcome is intended to be positive, making us more Christlike in our attitudes and actions.

However, the goal of shame is to convince us that something is intrinsically wrong with us that can't be fixed and for which there is no forgiveness. The end result is negative, robbing us of hope and filling us with despair.[5]

▶ **Shame** is a painful emotion of disgrace caused by a strong sense of guilt.

▶ **Shame** is experienced when our guilt moves from knowing we did something bad to feeling that we are bad.

► **Shame** focuses not on what we've done, but on being ashamed of who we are.

► **Shame** can cause us to feel like a failure—defective to the core—which causes a deep sense of unworthiness and a constant fear of rejection. Without emotional healing, these scars can last a lifetime.

In contrast, when we respond to our trials correctly, God gives us hope in place of shame.

> " ... we know that suffering produces perseverance; perseverance, character; and character, hope. And hope does not put us to shame, because God's love has been poured out into our hearts through the Holy Spirit, who has been given to us."
> (Romans 5:3–5)

Blame Shifting

QUESTION: "How can I overcome the guilt and shame I feel as a result of being blamed for the abuse perpetrated against me?"

ANSWER: Victimizers are notoriously skilled at blaming their abusive ways on those whom they abuse. Sadly, many wounded victims—due to their intense shame and vulnerability—fall prey to highly convincing perpetrators. However, no accusing words could be further from the truth.

► **Blame shifting is a tactic** used by verbal abusers to shift the appropriate blame from themselves (the guilty) to their victims (the innocent) in order to control others by using false guilt to break down any possibility of resistance.

▶ **No one makes another person sin.** In fact, you don't have the power to make another person sin. Your abuser alone is responsible for any sin against you.

▶ **No one deserves abuse;** therefore, you are not to blame for what was done to you. The shame belongs to the abuser alone, not to you.

> " ... shame will come on those
> who are treacherous without cause."
> (Psalm 25:3)

WHAT IS God's Heart on Guilt?

We don't have to be a "Judas" to be considered *guilty*.

In truth, no one has escaped being classified as *guilty*. From earliest childhood we experienced guilt when our little hearts were greedy and stole a cookie or when we first told a fib or when we deliberately disobeyed mom or dad. All of us have felt the guilt pangs of hurting someone dear to us, someone who trusted us. All of us have borne the guilt of gossiping about the failure of a "friend" or exaggerating an enemy's wrong—in an effort to minimize our own. And none of us has escaped the inner disappointment that comes with compromising our values and failing to right a wrong.

Every one of us has *been less* than we could have been and has *done less* than we could have done.

And every one of us has gone farther than we ever thought we'd go, stayed longer than we ever thought we'd stay, and paid more than we ever thought we'd pay in the pursuit of sin's pleasures.

Thus to varying degrees, we are all guilty—both of doing what was wrong and failing to do what was right. Rich and poor, young and old, educated and not, healthy and not, handsome and not, we are all equals when it comes to guilt. The Bible makes it clear:

> "There is no one on earth who is righteous,
> no one who does what is right
> and never sins."
> (Ecclesiastes 7:20)

The Bible sheds light on the purposes of God. His heart is to use our *true guilt* to fulfill His plan to restore His image in us, to adjust our attitudes and actions.

▶ **Guilt-free or guilt-ridden consciences** are given by God to persuade us that we are obeying or violating His will.

> *"They show that the requirements of the law are written on their hearts, their consciences also bearing witness, and their thoughts sometimes accusing them and at other times even defending them"* (Romans 2:15).

▶ **Guilt is universal**—the condition we all share, but God forgives and purifies those who confess their sins to Him.

"If we claim to be without sin, we deceive ourselves and the truth is not in us. If we confess our sins, he is faithful and just and will forgive us our sins and purify us from all unrighteousness" (1 John 1:8–9).

▶ **Guilt left unconfessed** and unforgiven brings painful consequences that God uses to discipline us.

"Why do you cry out over your wound, your pain that has no cure? Because of your great guilt and many sins I have done these things to you" (Jeremiah 30:15).

▶ **Guilt concealed** is harmful, but guilt confessed is met with mercy.

"Whoever conceals their sins does not prosper, but the one who confesses and renounces them finds mercy" (Proverbs 28:13).

▶ **Guilt used by God** causes us to confess our sins that He might forgive us.

"Then I acknowledged my sin to you and did not cover up my iniquity. I said, 'I will confess my transgressions to the LORD.' And you forgave the guilt of my sin" (Psalm 32:5).

▶ **Guilt is our condition** even if we are unaware of committing a sin. (If you unknowingly fail to reduce your driving speed through a school zone, you could still be fined by a policeman who states, "Ignorance of the law is no excuse.")

"If anyone sins and does what is forbidden in any of the LORD's commands, even though they do not know it, they are guilty and will be held responsible" (Leviticus 5:17).

▶ **Guilt can be cleansed only** through the sacrificial death of Christ.

"The law is only a shadow of the good things that are coming—not the realities themselves. For this reason it can never, by the same sacrifices repeated endlessly year after year, make perfect those who draw near to worship. Otherwise, would they not have stopped being offered? For the worshipers would have been cleansed once for all, and would no longer have felt guilty for their sins" (Hebrews 10:1–2).

▶ **Guilt cleansed by God** allows us to draw closer to Him.

"Let us draw near to God with a sincere heart and with the full assurance that faith brings, having our hearts sprinkled to cleanse us from a guilty conscience and having our bodies washed with pure water" (Hebrews 10:22).

Lack of Appropriate Guilt

QUESTION: **"I don't feel guilty when I do what I know is wrong, so what should I do?"**

ANSWER: First, acknowledging the truth that you have ongoing sin is a significant step. Now turn that truth into a prayer.

▶ "Lord, may I see my sin as You see it. May I hate my sin as You hate it."

▶ "Help me see when my heart has been hardened."

▶ "Help me feel the guilt I need in order to turn from my sin."

▶ "Help me face the wounds in my past to receive Your healing."

▶ "Thank You for removing the guilt of my sin as I confess it."

▶ "Empower me to walk in victory over this sin through your supernatural strength."

Realize, if you are doing what is right, you are where you need to be.

> "If you do what is right,
> will you not be accepted?
> But if you do not do what is right,
> sin is crouching at your door;
> it desires to have you,
> but you must rule over it."
> (Genesis 4:7)

CHARACTERISTICS

Nothing can change the choice he makes—the deed is done. Judas willingly betrays Jesus. But then *it* comes creeping in like a thief in the night.

The guilt of being a traitor punctures his pride and self-importance. Regret cuts through his conscience, ripping his moral fiber. *But this regret is without repentance*. For those who are sensitive to the conviction of sin, the first person they turn to is God Himself, sincerely confessing their sin and repenting in order to restore broken fellowship.

Judas feels profound guilt *with regret*, but sadly *without repentance*—thus, there's no redeeming end to his story. Judas never discovers the liberating joy of living *guilt free*. Therefore, the apostle Peter applies the following passage to the failed disciple:

"'May his place be deserted;
let there be no one to dwell in it' ...
'May another take his place of leadership.'"
(Acts 1:20)

He holds the unique distinction—the one and only disciple to double-cross the Savior of the world!

He has spent the last three years building his résumé: money manager, traveling companion, privileged apostle, only to see one choice change everything. Now he leaves a legacy tarnished with ignoble labels. Betrayer! Conspirator! Traitor!

Certainly, Jesus identifies with the heart cry of David in the Psalms:

> **"Even my close friend, someone I trusted,**
> **one who shared my bread,**
> **has turned against me."**
> **(Psalm 41:9)**

Though we may not be aware of it, in the deepest part of our being, we can function on the basis of buried, negative beliefs about ourselves. These beliefs become the basis for our behaviors and the dictator of our decisions.

Based on these unique roles, consider the following buried beliefs that can be clues to unresolved feelings of guilt even within ourselves![6]

▶ **The Loner**—"If you really knew me, you'd reject me and then *I'd feel guilty.*"

▶ **The Critic**—"I focus on the faults of others because if I looked at my own, *I'd feel guilty.*"

▶ **The Perfectionist**—"To be accepted, I can't make mistakes or *I'd feel guilty.*"

- ▶ **The Benefactor**—"I continually have to give gifts to others because if I don't, *I'd feel guilty.*"

- ▶ **The Penny Pincher**—"I mustn't spend money on clothes, gifts, or a nice place to eat because if I do, *I'd feel guilty.*"

- ▶ **The Martyr**—"I can't accept compliments or people will think I'm prideful and then *I'd feel guilty.*"

- ▶ **The Worrier**—"I worry about how to solve others' problems in order to prove that I care, but I won't focus on my failures or *I'd feel guilty.*"

- ▶ **The Iceberg**—"Because sex is 'dirty,' I can't respond to my spouse. If I did, *I'd feel guilty.*"

- ▶ **The Apologizer**—"I always apologize so that people won't have anger, because if they become angry with me, *I'd feel guilty.*"

- ▶ **The Defendant**—"My strongest defense is protecting myself, and without a defense, *I'd feel guilty.*"

- ▶ **The Confessor**—"If I admit guilt for everything, I can avoid feeling guilty about specific things. If I don't confess everything, *I'd feel guilty.*"

- ▶ **The Legalist**—"I have to do everything exactly by the book because if I failed in any area, *I'd feel guilty.*"

- ▶ **The Melancholic**—"If I remain depressed, I have an excuse for not facing my past. If I were to face my past, *I'd feel guilty.*"

Most of us have a hard time recognizing our blind spots and seeing ourselves in one of these "personalities." If you sincerely desire to know the truth about yourself, you must confront your inner enemies and be "set free." Consider asking trusted friends if they recognize any of these characteristics in you. Bridle your natural defenses and listen for God to speak the truth to you. His voice will be loving and gentle, communicating forgiveness, hope, and encouragement.

> "If we claim to be without sin,
> we deceive ourselves and the truth is not in us. If we confess our sins, he is faithful and just and will forgive us our sins
> and purify us from all unrighteousness."
> (1 John 1:8–9)

Deeply Buried Sins

QUESTION: "If I'm blind to the truth about myself, how can I know if I have deeply buried sins?

ANSWER: Trust God—He knows the hidden places of your heart.

▶ **Rely** on God to reveal the buried sins you are not aware of by praying: "Lord, reveal anything that is hidden from me that I need to deal with."

▶ **Realize**, God is more interested in your walking in truth than you are. He died so you could be set free from the power of sin in your life!

▶ **Rest** assured that He will reveal truth to anyone who earnestly seeks it.

The Word of God reminds us that nothing in our hearts is hidden from God.

"If we had forgotten the name of our God
or spread out our hands to a foreign god,
would not God have discovered it,
since he knows the secrets of the heart?"
(Psalm 44:20–21)

WHAT ARE Physical Ramifications of Unresolved Guilt?

A death sentence is pronounced for Jesus, and powerful emotions sweep over Judas—fear, anxiety, and guilt! They overwhelm him, as Scripture verifies, so that when he *"saw that Jesus was condemned, he was seized with remorse and returned the thirty pieces of silver to the chief priests and the elders. 'I have sinned,' he said, 'for I have betrayed innocent blood'"* (Matthew 27:3–4).

Judas, the world's most notorious traitor, never resolves his agonizing remorse. He never turns to God for help, for hope, or for healing. He instead takes matters into his own hands, committing an act that is not only vexing, *but also irreversible.*

"He went away and hanged himself."
(Matthew 27:5)

Both true guilt and false guilt need to be appropriately addressed and resolved. If we have difficulty detecting our own underlying guilt, we should look at the physical symptoms that are caused by unresolved guilt.[7]

- ▶ Anxiety
- ▶ Body shakes
- ▶ Cold sores
- ▶ Depression
- ▶ Easily fatigued
- ▶ Headaches
- ▶ Heart attack susceptibility
- ▶ High blood pressure
- ▶ Inability to relax
- ▶ Muscle tension
- ▶ Overweight
- ▶ Phobias
- ▶ Sexual impotency
- ▶ Sleeplessness
- ▶ Weakened immune system
- ▶ Ulcers

While many physical ailments are unrelated to guilt, some can be the direct result of guilt, as stated by the prophet Jeremiah:

> "Why do you cry out over your wound,
> your pain that has no cure?
> Because of your great guilt and many sins
> I have done these things to you."
> (Jeremiah 30:15)

Causes of Health Problems: Physical or Spiritual?

QUESTION: "How can I know whether my poor health has a physical or a spiritual root?"

ANSWER:

- ▶ First pray, "Lord, reveal to me the true cause of my health problems."

- ▶ Ask yourself, "Is there any unconfessed sin in my life?" (This isn't to produce guilt, but to pinpoint the cause because many reasons exist for illness.)

▶ If the answer is *yes*, then confess it and turn from it. Realize, the Lord can use guilt in your life— good guilt—to bring you into the light of His truth.

▶ Ask the elders of your church to pray for you. James 5:14 says, *"Is anyone among you sick? Let them call the elders of the church to pray over them and anoint them with oil in the name of the Lord."*

▶ Get a thorough medical examination.

▶ Do a biblical word study on sickness, illness, weakness, etc. to see what God's Word says. For example, the Bible warns that physical problems can be the result of spiritual failure.

"Whoever eats the bread or drinks the cup of the Lord in an unworthy manner will be guilty of sinning against the body and blood of the Lord. Everyone ought to examine themselves before they eat of the bread and drink from the cup. For those who eat and drink without discerning the body of Christ eat and drink judgment on themselves. That is why many among you are weak and sick, and a number of you have fallen asleep [meaning they died]." (1 Corinthians 11:27–30)

"Leave her alone" (John 12:7).

The words are Jesus' response to a critical comment spoken by Judas. The exchange occurs when Jesus is having dinner with three of his closest friends, Mary, Martha, and Lazarus. Suddenly Mary does something that draws feigned indignation from Judas—he pretends to be offended over the plight of the poor. While Jesus is reclining at a table, Mary pours about a pint of expensive perfume on Jesus' feet and then wipes His feet with her hair.

The lovely fragrance permeates the home, but Judas portrays it as an offense. *"Why wasn't this perfume sold and the money given to the poor? It was worth a year's wages"* (John 12:5).

More than likely, Judas is angry that the perfume hasn't been sold and the profits deposited into the disciples' money bag, because he is both "keeper" and "taker" of the bag. Judas *"was a thief; as keeper of the money bag, he used to help himself to what was put into it"* (John 12:6).

Jesus doesn't take the bait—He refuses to feel guilty when faced with Judas' criticism, nor is He fooled by Judas' fake piety. To the contrary, He turns the situation around and comes to Mary's defense.

"It was intended that she should save this perfume for the day of my burial. You will always have the poor among you, but you will not always have me."
(John 12:7–8)

Everyone on earth receives criticism, and everyone chooses a response. Life consists of a myriad of choices, and how we choose to deal with criticism is vital to our character. We can view criticism as a powerful enemy or as a potential friend to help us grow. Judas becomes negative; Jesus remains positive.

We can make something useful of it, or we can make something destructive of it. We can make a mountain of it, or make nothing of it. The choice is ours—likewise, the consequences are ours too.

Guilt-Ridden Reactions to Criticism

▶ **Discount** it totally

- Consider its source to be unknowledgeable and ignorant
- Consider it to be unworthy of the slightest consideration

▶ **Deny** its validity

- Declare it to be fabricated and completely unfounded
- Declare it to be an act of jealousy, a feeble attempt to ruin your reputation

▶ **Mount** a counterattack

- View it as a personal, malicious attack that cannot go unchallenged
- View it as a declaration of "war," which you will win at any cost

▶ **Have** an emotional meltdown

  ▪ Experience overwhelming feelings of anger, humiliation, embarrassment, rejection

  ▪ Experience uncontrolled crying, deep discouragement, resignation, depression

▶ **Accept** it blindly as being absolutely true

  ▪ Receive it as verification that all criticism you received as a child was totally justified

  ▪ Receive it as proof of your unworthiness and unacceptability

Instead of being deceived regarding the impact of unjust criticism, the Bible says ...

> "The wisdom of the prudent
> is to give thought to their ways,
> but the folly of fools is deception."
> (Proverbs 14:8)

Guilt-Free Reactions to Criticism

▶ **Objectively** evaluate it.

  ▪ Examine your mind, heart, and actions to find if there is any truthfulness in it.

  ▪ Examine yourself through the eyes of a close confidant and friend to determine whether it is based on truth or error.

▶ **Go to God** with it.

  ▪ Seek the truth by turning to God, asking Him to reveal truth to you.

- Seek the truth by turning to God's Word, evaluating yourself by the standard of God's Word.

▶ **Learn** from it.

- Determine to find a way to correct any attitude or action that needs to be improved.

- Determine to find a way to protect yourself from receiving any cruel, false criticism in the future.

▶ **Discard** it.

- Refuse to dwell on it or give it another thought—put it totally out of your mind.

- Refuse to give it any more credence, emotionally letting it go—consider it over and done.

▶ **Forgive** it.

- Release the critical words to God and forgive the pain they caused.

- Release the criticizer to God and forgive the offense.

Take to heart the fact that ...

> "A person may think their own ways are right, but the LORD weighs the heart."
> (Proverbs 21:2)

CAUSES OF GUILT

David stands out among God's anointed: a king described as a man after God's own heart. But a very dark season looms ahead—a season of his own making—when guilt suffocates all joy and strangles any semblance of peace.

David is a genuine servant of God, known for obeying the Word of God—a leader who has the blessing of God. But while David's reputation is "blameless," he is by no means sinless.

For almost an entire year sin so besets David that it seems inconceivable—how could he be the same king as described in the Bible as *"doing what was just and right for all his people"* (2 Samuel 8:15)?

During these darkest of times, David primarily sins against two people, a wife and her husband, but God sees the sins as a personal affront, which He clearly communicates to David through the prophet Nathan:

> "Why did you despise the word of the LORD by doing what is evil in his eyes?"
> (2 Samuel 12:9)

Guilt, more than any other emotion, can grab your heart, squeezing it with a death grip. Unfortunately, when we're in this tight grip, we can *feel guilty* when we're *not*. Therefore, when we have this flawed feeling, called *false guilt*, that doesn't mean we have disobeyed God or defied His moral laws.

In contrast, we need to feel *true guilt* by seeing ourselves squarely in the mirror so as to face our real sins, even our hidden faults for which we are accountable. David, who tried hard to hide his sin, later had this change of heart:

"Who can discern their own errors? Forgive my hidden faults. Keep your servant also from willful sins; may they not rule over me. Then will I be blameless, innocent of great transgression." (Psalm 19:12–13)

WHAT RUNS Your Life—Rules or Relationship?

The book of Psalms reveals much about David's intimacy with God as he pours out his heart before the Lord.

David, who wrote more than 70 of the 150 psalms, expresses heartfelt thanksgiving and hope-filled worship. But many of these psalms were written against a sullied background, depicting David's moral failure and imploring God's forgiveness. Notice his pleas for intervention and his prayers for deliverance.

When guilt wedged itself between this man and his God, their tender fellowship was broken. David had succumbed to temptation and entered into an adulterous affair with a beautiful woman named Bathsheba.

God is deeply grieved and angered by David's actions, but His love is too deep to even conceive of of cutting off a relationship with His sin-laden servant. David's sins are indeed great, but God's grace is all the greater.

> "The LORD has taken away your sin.
> You are not going to die."
> (2 Samuel 12:13)

Do you walk around with a master list of forbidden things in your mind? What does your list include? Many of us have a distorted perception of God. We see Him as a God of wrath, waiting to punish us when we step out of line or *break the rules*! If we see God as the "Great Punisher," our relationship with Him becomes one of fear and guilt rather than one of love and trust.

If our faith *increases guilt* rather than *decreases guilt*, we have a legalistic, rules-based relationship with God. However, the more we know the true character of God, the less guilt we will experience in relation to our own sin. The reason is this: The more we recognize God's undeserved forgiveness for our wrong choices—for our self-willed, self-centered choices—the more we will seek to please God by making choices that are right in His sight.

In light of our guilt, we feel all the more humbled when we focus on His love, unconditional grace and mercy—and yes, His full forgiveness. Through our life-changing relationship with the Lord, He says our sins are forgiven forever.

> "Blessed are those whose transgressions
> are forgiven, whose sins are covered."
> (Romans 4:7)

Rules-Based False Guilt[8]

I feel guilty when ...

▶ **I struggle** with overcoming a bad habit—even when I know I'm dealing with it.

▶ **I think** sexual thoughts—even when the thought is fleeting.

▶ **I spend** money for things I need—even when I have money to meet the need.

▶ **I get** angry—even when the anger is appropriate ("righteous indignation").

▶ **I can't** help everyone who asks—even when I'm not able to help.

▶ **I take** time off from work—even when I need to take the time.

▶ **I say** *no* to a spiritual leader—even when I'm not led by the Lord to say *yes*.

▶ **I am** tempted to sin—even when I choose not to sin.

▶ **I fail** to witness all the time—even when it's not the appropriate time.

The man Job, whom God called blameless, had friends who continued to blame him for all the tragedy that befell him—none of which was his own doing. Nevertheless, Job was so beaten down with accusations that he responded, *"If I am guilty—woe to me! Even if I am innocent, I cannot lift my head, for I am full of shame and drowned in my affliction"* (Job 10:15).

Stop Feeling Guilty

QUESTION: "I saw a friend steal something, and the next day I reported it. How can I not feel guilty for betraying my friend?"

ANSWER: If you failed to privately confront your friend before you reported the theft, then you are guilty of not providing your friend the opportunity to do the right thing and return the stolen item. In that case, your guilt is not that you reported the theft but that you did not first confront your friend.

However, if you did confront and the wrong was not righted, you were right to report the theft. Then, if you still feel guilty, you are feeling *false guilt*.

Consider this:

▶ Who is the one guilty of stealing? Your friend needs to feel true guilt.

▶ Anyone who is weak can keep silent after witnessing a theft, but it takes someone who is strong—a real friend of conscience—to speak up.

▶ Although you may not see it now, if your friend experiences a painful repercussion, you may have saved your friend from a lifestyle of stealing. The Bible says, *"A truthful witness saves lives ... "* (Proverbs 14:25).

You have acted wisely in seeking to know whether or not you have committed any sins so that you might correct any wrongs you may have done regarding your friend. Consider the words of righteous Job: *"How many wrongs and sins have I committed? Show me my offense and my sin"* (Job 13:23).

"You are the man!" (2 Samuel 12:7). The words are like a runaway freight train racing across David's conscience, unstoppable and completely on course toward *conviction*. This bold declaration demolishes David's stronghold of sinful secrets, affirming that the patience of God with His anointed king has worn out. David hasn't made the first move to confess his sins before God, so God makes the first move toward him.

The prophet Nathan is sent by God to present a parable to David, a story of injustice, shame, and contemptible selfishness. A rich man with numerous cattle and sheep prepares a meal for a traveler, but instead of slaughtering one of his own animals, he kills the one and only precious ewe that a poor man owns, a lamb that *"was like a daughter to him"* (2 Samuel 12:3).

David is incensed, declaring that the man deserves to die and must make restitution four times over, but then comes Nathan's righteous rebuke that he, the king, is indeed that man! David then recognizes that he is the story's main character. King David signifies an awareness of his true, blatant guilt with this sobering statement:

> **"I have sinned against the LORD."**
> **(2 Samuel 12:13)**

Sinned? Indeed! For months he planned and plotted the course of his sinful deeds. Remember when a younger David refused to lift his sword against a man (King Saul) who sought to kill him, yet now the older David orders the death of a man (Uriah) who risks his life to protect him. David is truly guilty, yet for months he skirted that fact. What caused him to suddenly realize his guilt, and where does guilt come from anyway? What is it's source?

▶ Source #1—The Conscience from God[9]

The God-given conscience provides us with the sense of right and wrong.

"For since the creation of the world God's invisible qualities—his eternal power and divine nature—have been clearly seen, being understood from what has been made, so that people are without excuse." (Romans 1:20)

Categories of the Conscience:

■ **Cognitive Conscience**—*insightful conscience*

"Do not conform to the pattern of this world, but be transformed by the renewing of your mind. Then you will be able to test and approve what God's will is—his good, pleasing and perfect will" (Romans 12:2).

■ **Convicting Conscience**—*ethical conscience*

"They show that the requirements of the law are written on their hearts, their consciences also bearing witness, and their thoughts sometimes accusing them and at other times even defending them" (Romans 2:15).

- **Cleansed Conscience**—*purified conscience*

"How much more, then, will the blood of Christ, who through the eternal Spirit offered himself unblemished to God, cleanse our consciences from acts that lead to death, so that we may serve the living God!" (Hebrews 9:14).

- **Clear Conscience**—*confident conscience*

" ... keeping a clear conscience, so that those who speak maliciously against your good behavior in Christ may be ashamed of their slander" (1 Peter 3:16).

- **Corrupt Conscience**—*impure conscience*

"To the pure, all things are pure, but to those who are corrupted and do not believe, nothing is pure. In fact, both their minds and consciences are corrupted" (Titus 1:15).

- **Calloused Conscience**—*seared conscience*

"Such teachings comes through hypocritical liars, whose consciences have been seared as with a hot iron" (1 Timothy 4:2).

QUESTION: "What is a seared conscience?"

ANSWER: A conscience that is dead—insensitive to the prodding of the Holy Spirit because of willful and repeated violations of God's will.

> "They claim to know God,
> but by their actions they deny him.
> They are detestable, disobedient
> and unfit for doing anything good."
> (Titus 1:16)

▶ **SOURCE #2—The Spirit of God**[10]

The Holy Spirit provides conviction when we are wrong to do what is right.

**"When he [the Holy Spirit] comes,
he will prove the world to be in the wrong
about sin and righteousness and judgment."
(John 16:8)**

- **The Holy Spirit** is a gift from God.

  "You will receive the gift of the Holy Spirit" (Acts 2:38).

- **The Holy Spirit** makes His home in your heart.

  "Do you not know that your bodies are temples of the Holy Spirit, who is in you, whom you have received from God?" (1 Corinthians 6:19).

- **The Holy Spirit** communicates God's love for you.

  " ... God's love has been poured out into our hearts through the Holy Spirit, who has been given to us" (Romans 5:5).

- **The Holy Spirit** writes God's laws on your heart.

  "The Holy Spirit also testifies to us about this. First he says: ' ... I will put my laws in their hearts, and I will write them on their minds'" (Hebrews 10:15–16).

- **The Holy Spirit** helps you understand the thoughts of God.

  " ... no one knows the thoughts of God except the Spirit of God" (1 Corinthians 2:11).

- **The Holy Spirit** teaches and reminds you of all things you have read and heard pertaining to God.

  "The Advocate, the Holy Spirit, whom the Father will send in my name, will teach you all things and will remind you of everything I have said to you" (John 14:26).

- **The Holy Spirit** confirms the truth within your conscience.

  " ... my conscience confirms it [the truth] through the Holy Spirit" (Romans 9:1).

- **The Holy Spirit** brings conviction to your heart.

  " ... because our gospel came to you ... with power, with the Holy Spirit and deep conviction" (1 Thessalonians 1:5).

- **The Holy Spirit** fills you with joy and peace and causes your life to overflow with hope!

  "May the God of hope fill you with all joy and peace as you trust in him, so that you may overflow with hope by the power of the Holy Spirit" (Romans 15:13).

- **The Holy Spirit** gives you the power to obey God and fulfill His purposes for you.

  "You will receive power when the Holy Spirit comes on you ... " (Acts 1:8).

Disobeying the Holy Spirit

QUESTION: "What happens when I disobey the prompting of the Holy Spirit?"

ANSWER: To disobey the prompting of the Holy Spirit is to reject the Holy Spirit. To reject the Holy Spirit is to reject God. Realize that disobedience always leads to discipline.

God intends to use the conviction of your guilt to lead you to confession and repentance so that He might have a restored relationship with you. Then, He will resume working in your life to refashion your character to reflect the character of Christ.

The Bible says ...

"Anyone who rejects this instruction does not reject a human being but God, the very God who gives you his Holy Spirit."
(1 Thessalonians 4:8)

For true Christians—believers in Jesus Christ—all sins have been forgiven, and God identifies them as *saints*, not sinners; as *sons* and *daughters*, not slaves.

Although Christians still sin, their primary identity is not based on *what they do*, but instead on *who they are*—they are adopted members of the family of God. Where David is concerned, he commits adultery and murder, but his primary identity before God is not "adulterer" and "murderer." David's primary identity is a dearly loved child of God.

For David—and all true believers—sin can never disrupt our *relationship* with the Lord, but it does disrupt our *fellowship* with Him if we don't confess our sins and repent. However, when we do, our relationship is restored and God chooses to remember our sins no more. False guilt can surface when we don't apply the promises of Scripture. Sadly, many Christians still feel guilty for sins that, in truth, God has long since forgotten. Put deep in your heart the following promise:

> **"For as high as the heavens are above the earth, so great is his love for those who fear him; as far as the east is from the west, so far has he removed our transgressions from us." (Psalm 103:11–12)**

The beginnings of false guilt go back to early childhood.[11] If you heard repeated messages saying, "you're naughty" or "you're bad," your heart began to whisper, *Shame on me!* The guilt moved from knowing you had done something bad to feeling that you are bad. Shame leads you to focus not on *what* you've done, but on being ashamed of *who you are*. These feelings then lead you to believe lies:

▶ "Love is based on my performance."

▶ "My performance does not live up to the expectations of others."

▶ "I will always be rejected and abandoned because I will never be good enough!"

Growing up hearing an inner voice saying, *Shame on me!* causes many of us to establish negative attitudes about ourselves. Unknown to us, we develop unhealthy patterns of relating to others that can last throughout adulthood. As these patterns develop, true guilt over an action that hurts another (real sorrow over our sin) is immediately transferred over to false guilt (fear of rejection from others).

"I was ashamed and humiliated because I bore the disgrace of my youth" (Jeremiah 31:19).

Reasons We Hold On to Guilt

In spite of all the negatives that go along with guilt, some people manage to find reasons to hold on to it as a way to use it to their advantage. Instead, these reasons work against those who need to benefit from guilt the way God designed it to be used—to be a blessing to us.

Some people hold on to guilt ...

▶ **To attract others**—Learning "social skills" in order to develop relationships is harder than connecting with people who have the same negative habits.

▶ **To avoid change**—Having to adjust to new ways of thinking and responding to truth is difficult.

▶ **To escape the scrutiny of others**—Acknowledging personal guilt often keeps others from feeling the need to confront, avoiding the pain of hearing their disapproval.

▶ **To divert attention from real problems**—Talking in general about guilt is less threatening than talking about the real core issues surrounding the guilt.

▶ **To get attention**—By sharing feelings of guilt, respect can be gained from those who admire a sensitive conscience, those who want to offer help.

▶ **To manipulate and control others**—Appearing to be overwhelmed with guilt serves to lower the expectations of others and reduces the possibility of being criticized or rejected.

▶ **To receive pity**—Sharing personal woes is a quick way to gain pity and sympathy from others, minimizing the probability of being confronted or challenged.

Those who seek to use guilt rather than depend on God to meet their needs would do well to heed the warning of the prophet Ezekiel: *"I the Lord have spoken. The time has come for me to act. I will not hold back; I will not have pity, nor will I relent. You will be judged according to your conduct and your actions, declares the Sovereign Lord"* (Ezekiel 24:14).

There's not a more personal, passage of Scripture than the prayer written by David concerning his own guilt. He admits his sin against Bathsheba and Uriah. He begins, *"Have mercy on me, O God, according to your unfailing love; according to your great compassion blot out my transgressions. Wash away all my iniquity and cleanse me from my sin"* (Psalm 51:1–2).

David expresses sorrow because he knows his sin—*all sin*—is first and foremost an affront against God. His lack of confession has resulted in the removal of blessing as well as deep emotional and spiritual pain. But later, David embraces the wonderful truths concerning God's forgiving love and restorative heart, and further writes ...

> **"Cleanse me with hyssop,**
> **and I will be clean; wash me,**
> **and I will be whiter than snow."**
> **(Psalm 51:7)**

Three God-Given Inner Needs

In reality, we have all been created with three God-given inner needs: for love, significance, and security.[12]

▶ **Love**—to know that someone is unconditionally committed to our best interest

"My command is this: Love each other as I have loved you" (John 15:12).

54

▶ **Significance**—to know that our lives have meaning and purpose

"I cry out to God Most High, to God who fulfills his purpose for me" (Psalm 57:2 ESV).

▶ **Security**—to feel accepted and a sense of belonging

"Whoever fears the LORD *has a secure fortress, and for their children it will be a refuge"* (Proverbs 14:26).

The Ultimate Need-Meeter

Why did God give us these deep inner needs, knowing that people fail people and self-effort fails us as well?

God gave us these inner needs so that we would come to know Him as our Need-Meeter. Our needs are designed by God to draw us into a deeper dependence on Christ. God did not create any person or position or any amount of power or possessions to meet the deepest needs in our lives. If a person or thing could meet all our needs, we would not need God! The Lord will use circumstances and bring positive people into our lives to be an extension of His care and compassion, but ultimately only God can satisfy all the needs of our hearts.

The Bible says ...

> **"The** LORD **will guide you always;**
> **he will satisfy your needs in a sun-scorched**
> **land and will strengthen your frame.**
> **You will be like a well-watered garden,**
> **like a spring whose waters never fail."**
> **(Isaiah 58:11)**

The apostle Paul reveals this truth by asking, *"What a wretched man I am. Who will rescue me from this body that is subject to death?"* Then answers his own question saying, *" ... Jesus Christ our Lord!"* (Romans 7:24–25).

All along, the Lord planned to meet our deepest needs for ...

▶ **Love**—*"I* [the Lord] *have loved you with an everlasting love; I have drawn you with unfailing kindness"* (Jeremiah 31:3).

▶ **Significance**—*"'For I know the plans I have for you,' declares the* LORD, *'plans to prosper you and not to harm you, plans to give you hope and a future'"* (Jeremiah 29:11).

▶ **Security**—*"The* LORD *himself goes before you and will be with you; he will never leave you nor forsake you. Do not be afraid; do not be discouraged"* (Deuteronomy 31:8).

In truth, our God-given needs for love, significance, and security are met legitimately in Christ Jesus! Philippians 4:19 makes it plain, *"My God will meet all your needs according to the riches of his glory in Christ Jesus."*

Development of Self-Effort

All of us emerge from childhood with inadequacies and failures, but when the heart is unmercifully controlled by shame, God-given inner needs are persistently met by self-effort.

▶ The need for **love** is met by pleasing others.

▶ The need for **significance** is met by perfect performance.

▶ The need for **security** is met by emotional dependencies.

"Am I now trying to win the approval of human beings, or of God? Or am I trying to please people? If I were still trying to please people, I would not be a servant of Christ" (Galatians 1:10).

Development of Wrong Beliefs

The root cause of false guilt is based on inaccurate feelings that have taken control of our thought process. These thinking patterns, and ultimately our major belief system, damage our concept of God and camouflage our need for a Savior.

> " ... I cannot lift my head, for I am full of shame and drowned in my affliction."
> (Job 10:15)

▶ **WRONG BELIEF:**

"The only way I'll be happy is to meet my own needs in my own way. I refuse to focus on guilt."

▶ **RIGHT BELIEF:**

"The only way I will overcome my guilt is to admit my unmet inner needs and to allow the Lord to meet my deepest needs for love, significance, and security."

"My God will meet all your needs according to the riches of his glory in Christ Jesus" (Philippians 4:19).

God created us with an innate need to have a loving relationship with Him. However, we've all been wrong. We've all been guilty. We've all violated the will of God.

And when we go against His will, a wall is erected between us and God—a spiritual separation. This wall called sin means choosing to go our own way instead of God's way, which results in growing, nagging guilt.

> **"Here we are before you [God] in our guilt, though because of it not one of us can stand in your presence."**
> **(Ezra 9:15)**

Why the Sacrificial Lamb of God?

We as *sinful* people need a *sinless* Savior, not only to die as the payment for our sins but also to become the strength to overcome our sins. Jesus is the only acceptable payment for our true guilt. Jesus is the only sufficient power source for victorious living.

The perfect sacrifice required in the Old Testament as a "guilt offering" for sin was a sacrificial lamb—a foreshadowing of Jesus Christ, the perfect sacrificial Lamb of God. Just as the lamb's blood was poured on the temple altar to secure the forgiveness of God, the shed blood of Christ on the cross covers your personal sins. When we receive Christ Jesus as our Lord and Savior, we are not only reconciled to God, but also made a child of God!

"The Spirit you received does not make you slaves, so that you live in fear again; rather, the Spirit you received brought about your adoption to sonship.
And by him we cry, 'Abba, Father.' ...
Because you are his sons, God sent the Spirit of his Son into our hearts, the Spirit who calls out, 'Abba, Father.'"
(Romans 8:15; Galatians 4:6)

Two questions beg to be asked of you:

▶ **Have you seen** your sin as God sees it?

▶ **Have you accepted** Christ's sacrifice on your behalf, trusting Him to be your personal guilt offering?

"All we like sheep have gone astray; we have turned—every one—to his own way; and the Lord *has laid on him the iniquity of us all. ... like a lamb that is led to the slaughter ... Yet it was the will of the* Lord *to crush him; he has put him to grief; when his soul makes an offering for guilt, he shall see his offspring; he shall prolong his days; the will of the* Lord *shall prosper in his hand."*
(Isaiah 53:6–7, 10 ESV)

Four Points of God's Plan

#1 God's Purpose for You is *Salvation.*

What was God's motivation in sending Jesus Christ to earth?

To express His love for you by saving you! The Bible says ...

"God so loved the world that he gave his one and only Son, that whoever believes in him shall not perish but have eternal life. For God did not send his Son into the world to condemn the world, but to save the world through him" (John 3:16–17).

What was Jesus' purpose in coming to earth?

To forgive your sins, to empower you to have victory over sin, and to enable you to live a fulfilled life! Jesus said ...

"I have come that they may have life, and that they may have it more abundantly" (John 10:10 NKJV).

#2 Your Problem is *Sin.*

What exactly is sin?

Sin is living independently of God's standard—knowing what is right, but choosing what is wrong. The Bible says ...

"If anyone, then, knows the good they ought to do and doesn't do it, it is sin for them" (James 4:17).

What is the major consequence of sin?

Spiritual death, eternal separation from God. Scripture states ...

"Your iniquities [sins] have separated you from your God. ... The wages of sin is death, but the gift of God is eternal life in Christ Jesus our Lord" (Isaiah 59:2; Romans 6:23).

#3 God's Provision for You is the *Savior*.

Can anything remove the penalty for sin?

Yes! Jesus died on the cross to personally pay the penalty for your sins. The Bible says ...

"God demonstrates his own love for us in this: While we were still sinners, Christ died for us" (Romans 5:8).

What is the solution to being separated from God?

Belief in (entrusting your life to) Jesus Christ as the only way to God the Father. Jesus says ...

"I am the way and the truth and the life. No one comes to the Father except through me. ... Believe in the Lord Jesus, and you will be saved ... " (John 14:6; Acts 16:31).

#4 Your Part is *Surrender*.

Give Christ control of your life, entrusting yourself to Him.

"Jesus said to his disciples, 'Whoever wants to be my disciple must deny themselves and take up their cross [die to your own self-rule] and follow me. For whoever wants to save their life will lose it, but whoever loses their life for me will find it. What good will it be for someone to gain the whole world, yet forfeit their soul?'" (Matthew 16:24–26).

Place your faith in (rely on) Jesus Christ as your personal Lord and Savior and reject your "good works" as a means of earning God's approval.

"It is by grace you have been saved, through faith—and this is not from yourselves, it is the gift of God—not by works, so that no one can boast" (Ephesians 2:8–9).

The moment you choose to receive Jesus as your Lord and Savior—entrusting your life to Him—He comes to live inside you. Then He gives you His power to live the fulfilled life God has planned for you. If you want to be fully forgiven by God and become the person God created you to be, you can tell Him in a simple, heartfelt prayer like this:

PRAYER OF SALVATION

*God, I want a real relationship with You.
I admit that many times I've failed
to go Your way and instead
chosen to go my own way.
Please forgive me for my sins.
Jesus, thank You for dying on the cross
to pay the penalty for my sins
and for rising from the dead to provide new
life. Come into my life to be my Lord and my
Savior. Place Your hope in my heart
and teach me to put my confidence in You.
Make me the person You created me to be.
In Your holy name I pray. Amen.*

What Can You Expect Now?

If you sincerely prayed this prayer, look at what God says about you!

"His divine power has given us everything we need for a godly life ... "
(2 Peter 1:3)

STEPS TO SOLUTION

" ... he went into the house of the LORD and worshiped." (2 Samuel 12:20)

This act of remorse and repentance signals a contrite heart and a will surrendered to the sovereign plan of God. David's sins against Bathsheba and her husband have been forgiven. But there are tragic consequences for his conduct that stretch throughout the remainder of his life.

The prophet Nathan makes a disastrous proclamation ... one that brings the King of Israel to his knees ... but ultimately David's moving act of worship signifies a changed, repentant heart. And that is precisely David's plea in Psalm 51:

"Create in me a pure heart, O God,
and renew a steadfast spirit within me."
(Psalm 51:10)

Spiritual brokenness does not *destroy* value—it *increases* value. A wild horse whose will is not broken, who has not yet submitted to its rider has no useful value to its owner. But a broken horse becomes more and more valuable as he becomes trained and responds to the slightest tug on the reins. God shows His delight in a heart broken over sin and a will that is broken and yielded to the Savior.

"My sacrifice, O God, is a broken spirit;
a broken and contrite heart you, God, will
not despise." (Psalm 51:17)

Key Verse to Memorize

Psalm 32:5, written by David, indicates his acknowledgement and confession of sin and the full forgiveness from God that grants David the privilege of living without the guilt of his past, as well as giving the gift of an eternity in heaven.

But there *is* an immediate catastrophic consequence from his previous sinful behavior. Bathsheba has just given birth to a son, and Nathan pronounces: " ... *the son born to you will die*" (2 Samuel 12:14). David pleads with God, refuses to eat, and "[spends] *the nights lying in sackcloth on the ground*" (2 Samuel 12:16). But on the seventh day, the son dies.

> **"Then I acknowledged my sin to you**
> **and did not cover up my iniquity.**
> **I said, 'I will confess my transgressions to**
> **the LORD.' And you forgave**
> **the guilt of my sin."**
> **(Psalm 32:5)**

Key Passage to Read

King David's reign came about 1,000 years before Christ, but Jesus' death and resurrection has as much impact for David as it does for us today.

Christ freely gives the "guilt offering" to pay the price for our sins. His precious blood alone can cleanse us from unrighteousness. And the power of that shed blood to make atonement is effective for all who believe in God by faith. Jesus, as our guilt offering, covers all the sins of those who accept His gift.

Hebrews 10:1–23

The Old Testament Guilt Offering

▶ Old Testament sacrifices were a picture of the perfect sacrifice (Christ) that was to come. (v. 1)

  ▪ Old Testament sacrifices were never able to make people perfect. (v. 1)

▶ Old Testament sacrifices never cleansed people once for all or removed their feelings of guilt. (v. 2)

  ▪ Old Testament sacrifices were only reminders of sins, not the remedy for sin. (v. 3)

▶ It is impossible for the blood of animals to take away sins. (v. 4)

  ▪ The body of Christ is the only true sacrifice for the forgiveness of sin. (vv. 5–7)

▶ Old Testament priests performed their rituals day after day. (v. 11)

  ▪ Again and again, such sacrifices could never take away sin. (v. 11)

The New Testament Sacrificial Savior

▶ But God's Son offered a onetime sacrifice for all. (v. 12)

  ▪ He sat down at the right hand of the Father. (v. 12)

▶ Since that time, He waits for His enemies to be humbled. (v. 13)

  ▪ For by one sacrifice, He made perfect those who are becoming holy. (v. 14)

▶ The Holy Spirit testifies to all of us about what He has said. (v. 15)

  ▪ "I will put my laws on their hearts and their minds." (v. 16)

▶ "Their sins and lawless acts I will remember no more." (v. 17)

  ▪ And where these are forgiven, no longer is sacrifice necessary. (v. 18)

Epilogue

▶ We now have confidence to enter the Most Holy Place by the blood of Jesus. (v. 19)

▶ By the new way of God's grace, the curtain (His Body) is opened for us. (v. 20)

▶ With full assurance through faith, let's draw near to God, having our guilt washed away. (v. 22)

▶ And let us cling to the hope that is ours, for He who has promised is faithful. (v. 23)

Nothing compares with the absolute assurance that our sins have been atoned for—forgiven—forever erased from God's book of records! Knowing this truth brings joy to our hearts. No longer must we carry the weight of the world on our backs. Now we can set our sights on a new target, focus on a new plan, and begin a deeper walk with God—a walk unencumbered by unresolved guilt, with a conscience clear before God.

"Let us draw near to God with a sincere heart and with the full assurance that faith brings, having our hearts sprinkled to cleanse us from a guilty conscience and having our bodies washed with pure water." (Hebrews 10:22)

Reaching the Target

▶ **Target #1—A New Purpose**: God's purpose for me is to be conformed to the character of Christ.

"Those God foreknew he also predestined to be conformed to the image of his Son ... " (Romans 8:29).

- "I'll do whatever it takes to be conformed to the character of Christ."

▶ **Target #2—A New Priority**: God's priority for me is to change my thinking.

"Do not conform to the pattern of this world, but be transformed by the renewing of your mind" (Romans 12:2).

- "I'll do whatever it takes to line up my thinking with God's thinking.

▶ **Target #3—A New Plan**: God's plan for me is to rely on Christ's strength, not my strength, to be all He created me to be.

"I can do all things through him who strengthens me" (Philippians 4:13 ESV).

- "I'll do whatever it takes to fulfill His plan in His strength."

My Personalized Plan

In the strength of Christ, I will continually seek to walk before God with a clear conscience, confronting both true and false guilt on a daily basis and taking the necessary steps to rid myself of false guilt and to avoid sin, the cause of true guilt.

"So I strive always to keep my conscience clear before God and man."
(Acts 24:16)

▶ **I will acknowledge** the existence and prevalence of guilt in my life.

- Identify specific areas in which I am prone to experience guilt

- Clarify how often and the degree to which I feel guilt

"For troubles without number surround me; my sins have overtaken me, and I cannot see. They are more than the hairs of my head, and my heart fails within me" (Psalm 40:12).

▶ **I will ascertain** the sources of my guilt.

- Discern if my guilty feelings are related to rules and regulations from childhood, church, or culture

- Determine if my guilt is the result of failing to meet God's, someone else's, or my own expectations of me

"Do not bring your servant into judgment, for no one living is righteous before you" (Psalm 143:2).

▶ **I will admit** the ineffective ways I address my guilt.

- Honestly evaluate whether I constantly deny, analyze, ignore, mask, suppress, cover, disguise, or surrender to my feelings of guilt

- Realistically asses whether I deal with guilt by justifying it, pretending it doesn't exist, getting angry, avoiding people and places, blaming others, becoming legalistic, or doing good deeds in an attempt to atone for my sins

"The heart of the discerning acquires knowledge, for the ears of the wise seek it out" (Proverbs 18:15).

▶ **I will confront** my true guilt and guilty feelings.

- Admit and accept the fact that sin residing within me makes sin inevitable and inescapable, and makes guilt prevalent and perpetual

- Embrace the fact of my guilt and reject the feelings of guilt, rejoicing in the forgiving, redeeming, loving arms of God, who cleanses, empowers, and transforms me into His likeness

"For I know that good itself does not dwell in me, that is, in my sinful nature. For I have the desire to do what is good, but I cannot carry it out. ... Thanks be to God, who delivers me through Jesus Christ our Lord! So then, I myself in my mind am a slave to God's law, but in my sinful nature a slave to the law of sin" (Romans 7:18, 25).

▶ **I will differentiate** between true and false guilt.

- Read, study, memorize, meditate on, and teach God's Word so that I might know Him well enough to recognize when I have sinned against Him and then experience true guilt

- Examine possible wrong beliefs I have that might be producing guilty feelings in me once I know I have not sinned

"I have hidden your word in my heart that I might not sin against you" (Psalm 119:11).

▶ **I will reject** false guilt.

- Replace wrong beliefs leading to false guilt with new beliefs based on biblical truth

- Ask God to keep me alert to false guilt operating in me and to point out areas where I am vulnerable to accepting blame that is misplaced

"See if there is any offensive way in me, and lead me in the way everlasting" (Psalm 139:24).

▶ **I will respond** to true guilt.

- Identify sin that leads to guilt feelings; respond to the Holy Spirit's conviction; repent and renounce my sin; acknowledge and confess my sins to God and relevant others; seek forgiveness from God and others

- Make restitution when appropriate; seek reconciliation when appropriate; commit to making needed changes in attitude and/ or behavior; accept and rejoice over being forgiven; make a God-directed plan to establish a new behavior pattern

"I will instruct you and teach you in the way you should go; I will counsel you with my loving eye on you" (Psalm 32:8).

HOW TO Distinguish True Guilt from False Accusation

True guilt brings righteous conviction to David's life, and *true guilt* develops inner character in the man of God once enmeshed in sin.

Following the death of his son with Bathsheba, David's servants are afraid to tell the king the tragic news because they fear—*"He may do something desperate"* (2 Samuel 12:18). David senses the baby's death has occurred, gets confirmation from his servants, and then manifests a remarkable change of demeanor. His next actions are a moving testimony to a man who totally surrenders to the sovereign will of God *even when it involves great pain.* David gets up from the ground, and *"after he had washed, put on lotions and changed his clothes, he went into the house of the LORD and worshiped"* (2 Samuel 12:20).

Although God may *convict* us of wrong behavior, He is not the author of condemning and unworthy feelings associated with guilt. *God's conviction* is a prompting in our hearts to change inappropriate behavior for a more Christlike response. If you know you are forgiven and you have confessed your sins to clear your conscience and restore fellowship with God, then see God's conviction as His call for action to change. Understand that He extends the grace of *total forgiveness* toward you. The Bible gives you this assurance:

> **"When you were dead in your sins**
> **and in the uncircumcision of your flesh,**
> **God made you alive with Christ.**
> **He forgave us all our sins."**
> **(Colossians 2:13)**

As you seek to distinguish true guilt from false accusation, remember ...

▶ **True Guilt** speaks with conviction, reminding us that we are all guilty of sin.

False Accusation: "I feel like a failure and not as worthy as others."

"All have sinned and fall short of the glory of God" (Romans 3:23).

▶ **True Guilt** is concerned about developing your inner character.

False Accusation: "I worry about how I am looking in the eyes of others."

"The LORD does not look at the things people look at. People look at the outward appearance, but the LORD looks at the heart" (1 Samuel 16:7).

▶ **True Guilt** communicates God's love, concern, and encouragement to you.

False Accusation: "I feel humiliated when I do something wrong."

"Because of the LORD's great love we are not consumed, for his compassions never fail. They are new every morning; great is your faithfulness" (Lamentations 3:22–23).

▶ **True Guilt** does not make excuses for itself.

False Accusation: "I feel I can't be healed … that I'm a victim of my past."

"Have mercy on me, LORD; heal me, for I have sinned against you" (Psalm 41:4).

▶ **True Guilt** allows for failure.

False Accusation: "I feel like I'll never measure up because of my repeated failures."

"Simon, Simon, Satan has asked to sift all of you as wheat. But I have prayed for you, Simon, that your faith may not fail. And when you have turned back, strengthen your brothers" (Luke 22:31–32).

▶ **True Guilt** encourages your real feelings to surface.

False Accusation: "I feel I must never become angry."

"'In your anger do not sin': Do not let the sun go down while you are still angry" (Ephesians 4:26).

▶ **True Guilt** is accompanied by a desire for you to change.

False Accusation: "I feel like there is no hope for me to change.

"I desire to do your will, my God ... My hope is in you" (Psalm 40:8; 39:7).

▶ **True Guilt** lifts your spirits when you are in prayer with God.

False Accusation: "I feel down and depressed—God doesn't hear my prayers."

"I ... will praise your name for your unfailing love and your faithfulness ... When I called, you answered me; you gently emboldened me" (Psalm 138:2–3).

▶ **True Guilt** is optimistic about the future.

False Accusation: "I feel that something bad is sure to happen to me in the future."

"'For I know the plans I have for you,' declares the LORD, 'plans to prosper you and not to harm you, plans to give you hope and a future'" (Jeremiah 29:11).

My Inner Voice

QUESTION: "How can I know if the inner voice I'm hearing is God's loving conviction of sin or Satan's false accusations?"

ANSWER: Be willing to search out both the behavior and your motives for the behavior that produced the possible guilt. Ask God to give you insight into both and to teach you to recognize what is truly from the Holy Spirit. Realize that God has given you His Word to reveal His thoughts and ways to you. The more you study His Word, the more likely you will correctly identify His voice when He speaks to you.

"Whether you turn to the right or to the left,
your ears will hear a voice behind you,
saying, 'This is the way; walk in it.'"
(Isaiah 30:21)

HOW TO Recognize Your Spiritual Enemy

David writes passionate words of remorse—words of regret and words of repentance. And he conveys a genuine understanding of the full forgiveness available to him. But David could have heard the enemy's voice reminding him of his failure.

The voice of the enemy has been wreaking havoc on the crowning glory of God's creation since the Garden of Eden. He misled and lied to Adam and Eve, and Satan still today tries to mislead and lie to God's people.

Satan whispers and he wounds. He discourages and he devastates.

God's judgment of David's sins, as well as His judgment of all believers' sins, fell squarely and completely on Jesus. The penalty demanded by that judgment was **paid in full**. Those three words always silence the voice of the enemy.

> " ... Put your hope in the LORD,
> for with the LORD is unfailing love
> and with him is full redemption."
> (Psalm 130:7)

Know that Satan tenaciously incriminates committed Christians, using guilt and fear to bring spiritual discouragement. Learn to discern the lies of Satan. He often communicates with a subtle use of unreasonable "should's."

Beware of "You should ...

▶ "**Be smarter** and more capable."

▶ "**Be happy** all the time."

▶ "**Be wealthy** and grow rich."

▶ "**Be able to do** whatever people ask you to do."

▶ "**Be able to never** have anger."

▶ "**Be able to cover up** your real feelings."

▶ "**Be able to hide** your tears."

▶ "**Be able to disguise** your weakness."

▶ "**Be the perfect** child, friend, mate, parent, employee ... person."

Find encouragement from God's Word:

**"The accuser of our brothers and sisters,
who accuses them before our God
day and night, has been hurled down."
(Revelation 12:10)**

And always remain on guard because …

**" … Satan himself masquerades as an angel
of light." (2 Corinthians 11:14)**

**" … there is no truth in him. When he lies,
he speaks his native language,
for he is a liar and the father of lies."
(John 8:44)**

HOW TO Resolve to Forgive Yourself

Undoubtedly, David seeks forgiveness from God, but the next order of business is for David to forgive himself.

God does not desire that we live our lives buried under a load of guilt. He wants to lift that load so we can become all He created us to be. But if we can't move past our past, how can we move forward into our future?

And God has big plans for David: His lineage will not only include the wisest king who ever lived, but also the *King of Kings and Lord of Lords, Jesus Christ.* The Gospel of Matthew opens …

**"This is the genealogy of Jesus the Messiah
the son of David, the son of Abraham."
(Matthew 1:1)**

Make the choice now to accept the truth that the penalty for your sins was long ago settled by Jesus' death on the cross.

Consider your answers to these questions:

▶ **How many of your sins** did Jesus die for before you were born? _____

▶ **How many of your sins** were in the future when Jesus died on the cross? _____

▶ **How many of your sins** did God know about before you were born? _____

▶ **How many of your sins** did Christ know you would commit after becoming a Christian? _____

▶ **How many of your sins** did Jesus pay for on the cross? _____

Although some sins bring greater consequences than others, God's viewpoint is that sin is sin. When we confess and repent based on our faith in Christ, His forgiveness covers all of our sins— and that includes *every* sin! Yet some of us place ourselves above God and become unwilling to forgive ourselves. Nowhere in the Bible does God say He forgives all our sins except (<u>fill in the blank</u>)!

If you choose to have a self-focused, unforgiving heart, you will struggle with ...

▶ **Uncertainty** about where you stand before God

▶ **Undesired** compulsive behavior

▶ **Unspiritual** false humility

▶ **Undeserved** self-deprivation

▶ **Unawareness** of God's priorities for you

▶ **Undervalued** sense of your usefulness to God

"This is how we know that we belong to the
truth and how we set our hearts at rest
in his presence: If our hearts condemn
us, we know that God is greater than our
hearts, and he knows everything.
Dear friends, if our hearts do not condemn
us, we have confidence before God
and receive from him anything we ask,
because we keep his commands
and do what pleases him."
(1 John 3:19–22)

Certainly, you would never consider yourself to be in a higher position of authority than God, yet that is what you do when you refuse to forgive yourself. Because the Lord has forgiven you through Christ, He expects you to forgive others—including yourself.

"Bear with each other and forgive one
another if any of you has a grievance
against someone.
Forgive as the Lord forgave you."
(Colossians 3:13)

David needs no better proof that God forgives and forgets than what happens immediately following the death of his and Bathsheba's first son.

"Then David comforted his wife Bathsheba, and he went to her and made love to her. She gave birth to a son, and they named him Solomon. The LORD loved him; and because the LORD loved him, he sent word through Nathan the prophet to name him Jedidiah" (2 Samuel 12:24–25).

David and Bathsheba's second son thus is double-named: Solomon means "peace," and Jedidiah means "loved by the Lord." David and Bathsheba's choosing of a name that means peace perhaps speaks that the pair are now living guilt free—they truly have found peace with God. And the name Jedidiah hints that God has made his choice for the successor to David's throne.

"God gave Solomon wisdom and very great insight, and a breadth of understanding as measureless as the sand on the seashore" (1 Kings 4:29).

Do you remember falling down and scraping your knee as a child? Did you run to your mother for her to pick you up and kiss the hurt away? Miraculously, it always worked! You felt good again and ran back out to play. The same is true when we take our bruised and broken lives to God: He forgives and forgets! It always works! And when we trust Him, He takes away all the guilt!

"When Jesus saw their faith, he said, 'Friend, your sins are forgiven'" (Luke 5:20).

God gives us this faithful promise:

> **"I, even I, am he who blots out your transgressions, for my own sake, and remembers your sins no more."**
> **(Isaiah 43:25)**

The following is an acrostic of the word FORGIVEN.

Find the source of your guilt.

▶ Examine why you are feeling guilty.

▶ Determine if your guilt is true or false.

▶ Use Scripture as the only standard for determining true guilt.

"You desired faithfulness even in the womb; you taught me wisdom in that secret place" (Psalm 51:6).

Own responsibility for your sin.

▶ Agree with God that you are guilty of sinning.

▶ Ask God to reveal your own personal sin patterns.

▶ Make restitution to those whom you have sinned against.

"Have mercy on me, O God, according to your unfailing love; according to your great compassion blot out my transgressions. Wash away all my iniquity and cleanse me from my sin. For I know my transgressions, and my sin is always before me. Against you, you only, have I

sinned and done what is evil in your sight; so you are right in your verdict and justified when you judge" (Psalm 51:1–4).

Realize that God means what He says.

> ▶ Thank God for the gift of His Son, who paid for your forgiveness.

> ▶ Thank God for His unending forgiveness, even if you don't feel forgiven.

> ▶ Choose to believe what God says.

"In him we have redemption through his blood, the forgiveness of sins, in accordance with the riches of God's grace that he lavished on us." (Ephesians 1:7–8).

Give up dwelling on the past.

> ▶ Give up holding on to past pain.

> ▶ Give up self-condemnation.

> ▶ Give up refusing to forgive others.

"Forget the former things; do not dwell on the past" (Isaiah 43:18).

Invest time in renewing your mind.

> ▶ Memorize Scripture that reinforces God's forgiveness.

> ▶ Remember that "in Christ you are a new creation" (2 Corinthians 5:17).

> ▶ Learn to see yourself as a valuable child of God.

"You were taught, with regard to your former way of life, to put off your old self, which is being corrupted by its deceitful desires; to be made new in the attitude of your minds" (Ephesians 4:22–23).

Verify truth when Satan accuses.

  ▶ Learn to discern the difference between the Holy Spirit's voice and that of Satan.

  ▶ Answer Satan's accusations with truth from Scripture.

  ▶ Verbalize a personal prayer receiving God's forgiveness.

"'No weapon forged against you will prevail, and you will refute every tongue that accuses you. This is the heritage of the servants of the LORD, and this is their vindication from me,' declares the LORD" (Isaiah 54:17).

Exchange your life for the life of Christ.

  ▶ Understand that you cannot live the Christian life in your own strength.

  ▶ Allow Christ to transform you and live out His character through you.

  ▶ Continue to yield to the Holy Spirit's direction through personal prayer and Bible study.

"I have been crucified with Christ and I no longer live, but Christ lives in me. The life I now live in the body, I live by faith in the Son of God, who loved me and gave himself for me" (Galatians 2:20).

Notice that God brings your feelings in line with the facts when you obey Him.

▶ Know God as a God of second chances!

▶ Know that your feelings won't change immediately.

▶ Know that feelings usually follow thinking.

"You need to persevere so that when you have done the will of God, you will receive what he has promised" (Hebrews 10:36).

"Blessed is the one
whose transgressions are forgiven,
whose sins are covered.
Blessed is the one whose sin the LORD
does not count against them
and in whose spirit is no deceit."
(Psalm 32:1–2)

The life of David serves as an excellent example that the grace of God is greater than all our guilt and that living guilt free is possible because of Jesus' sacrifice for our sins.

Sadly, many Christians who know that God has forgiven them still feel weighed down with guilt and self-condemnation. Jesus invites those who are burdened to come to Him and receive His rest.

> **"Come to me, all you who are weary and burdened, and I will give you rest."**
> **(Matthew 11:28)**

God's Spirit Can Succeed Where You Have Failed

If self-condemnation is your burden, memorize the following passages of Scriptures.

▶ **"God has forgiven me."**

"Whoever conceals their sins does not prosper, but the one who confesses and renounces them finds mercy" (Proverbs 28:13).

▶ **"God has purified me."**

"If we walk in the light, as he is in the light, we have fellowship with one another, and the blood of Jesus, his Son, purifies us from all sin" (1 John 1:7).

▶ **"God will not remember my sin."**

"I will forgive their wickedness and will remember their sins no more" (Hebrews 8:12).

▶ **"God will not bring a charge against me."**

"Who will bring any charge against those whom God has chosen? It is God who justifies. Who then is the one who condemns? No one. Christ Jesus, who died—more than that, who was raised to life—is at the right hand of God and is also interceding for us" (Romans 8:33–34).

▶ **"God has given me a personal guarantee."**

"Though your sins are like scarlet, they shall be as white as snow; though they are red as crimson, they shall be like wool" (Isaiah 1:18).

▶ **"God has freed me from my past."**

"Forget the former things; do not dwell on the past. See, I am doing a new thing! Now it springs up; do you not perceive it? I am making a way in the wilderness and streams in the wasteland" (Isaiah 43:18–19).

▶ **"God does not condemn me."**

"Whoever believes in him is not condemned ... " (John 3:18).

▶ **"God gives me peace."**

"Since we have been justified through faith, we have peace with God through our Lord Jesus Christ" (Romans 5:1).

Personal Prayer

"Dear Heavenly Father,
You know the heaviness I've carried in my heart
because of my guilt. I admit that many times I've
had wrong attitudes and wrong actions.
I know I've been self-willed
and I haven't lived according to Your will.
Thank You for using "good guilt" to let me know I
was going the wrong way and to convince me that I
needed to go the right way.

I realize that You paid the penalty
I should have paid for the guilt of my sin.
Please forgive me for all my sins.

Lord Jesus, thank You for loving me.
Thank You for Your mercy toward me.
Thank You for dying on the cross for me.

Now I ask You to come into my life
to be my Lord and Savior.
I give You control over every part of my life.

May I see my sin as You see it.
May I hate my sin as You hate it.

Please guide me to know when I'm feeling
false guilt instead of true guilt.

Help me lay aside all my feelings of false guilt
and self-condemnation. Keep my heart focused
on following Your Holy Spirit.

Thank You that I'm forgiven and set free.
In Jesus' holy name I pray, Amen."

*Guilt is a self-imposed prison
when granted residence in you.*

—June Hunt

SCRIPTURES TO MEMORIZE

Is everyone a sinner? Is there anyone who is **without sin**?

> *"Who can say, 'I have kept my heart pure; I am clean and **without sin**'?"* (Proverbs 20:9)

Can the good outweigh the bad—can my **righteous acts** outweigh the wrong that I've done?

> *"All of us have become like one who is unclean, and all our **righteous acts** are like filthy rags; we all shrivel up like a leaf, and like the wind our sins sweep us away."* (Isaiah 64:6)

Since God knows each time we have **turned to our own way**, what provision has He made for our sins?

> *"We all, like sheep, have gone astray, each of us has **turned to our own way**; and the LORD has laid on him the iniquity of us all."* (Isaiah 53:6)

Will I face **condemnation** for the sins I've committed after becoming a Christian?

> *"There is now no **condemnation** for those who are in Christ Jesus."* (Romans 8:1)

What is the consequence for the one who **conceals their sins** as opposed to the one who **confesses them**?

> *"Whoever **conceals their sins** does not prosper, but the one who **confesses** and renounces **them** finds mercy."* (Proverbs 28:13)

How can I have the confidence of knowing that **the Lord forgave the guilt of my sin**?

> *"I acknowledged my sin to you and did not cover up my iniquity. I said, 'I will confess my transgressions to **the Lord**.' And you **forgave the guilt of my sin**."* (Psalm 32:5)

Although I know I've been forgiven, can I have confidence that God will **remember** my **sins no more**?

> *"'Their **sins** and lawless acts I will **remember no more**.' And where these have been forgiven, sacrifice for sin is no longer necessary."* (Hebrews 10:17–18)

What is the difference between **godly sorrow** and being sorry that I got caught?

> *"**Godly sorrow** brings repentance that leads to salvation and leaves no regret, but worldly sorrow brings death."* (2 Corinthians 7:10)

What should I do if I confess my sin, but still have a **guilty conscience**?

> *"Let us draw near to God with a sincere heart and with the full assurance that faith brings, having our hearts sprinkled to cleanse us from a **guilty conscience** and having our bodies washed with pure water."* (Hebrews 10:22)

What can I do to **keep my conscience clear**?

> *"I strive always to **keep my conscience clear** before God and man."* (Acts 24:16)

NOTES

1. Bruce Narramore and Bill Counts, *Freedom from Guilt* (Eugene, OR: Harvest House, 1974), 34–37.

2. Robert Laird Harris, Gleason Leonard Archer, Bruce K. Waltke, *Theological Wordbook of the Old Testament*, electronic ed. (Chicago: Moody Press, 1999), s.v. TWOT# 180.

3. Brent Curtis, *Guilt*, Institute for Biblical Counseling Discussion Guide, ed. Tom Varney (Colorado Springs, CO: NavPress, 1992), 14–15, 17, 19, 24.

4. Adapted from Robert S. McGee, *The Search for Significance*: Book & Workbook, 2nd ed. (Houston, TX: Rapha, 1990), 168–170.

5. Curtis, *Guilt*, 18–19, 21.

6. Narramore and Counts, *Freedom from Guilt*, 11-18.

7. Jay Edward Adams, *The Christian Counselor's Manual* (Grand Rapids: Baker, 1973), 463 and Gary R. Collins, *Christian Counseling: A Comprehensive Guide*, rev. ed. (Dallas: Word, 1988), 141.

8. Becca Cowan Johnson, *Good Guilt, Bad Guilt: And What to Do with Each* (Downer's Grove: InterVarsity Press, 1996), 68-75.

9. J. Dwight Pentecost, *Man's Problems—God's Answers* (Chicago: Moody, 1971), 11–17.

10. Pentecost, *Man's Problems*, 17–23.

11. Narramore and Counts, *Freedom from Guilt*, 21–22, 24–25.

12. Lawrence J. Crabb, Jr., *Understanding People: Deep Longings for Relationship*, Ministry Resources Library (Grand Rapids: Zondervan, 1987), 15–16; Robert S. McGee, *The Search for Significance*, 2nd ed. (Houston, TX: Rapha, 1990), 27–30.

SELECTED BIBLIOGRAPHY

Adams, Jay Edward. *The Christian Counselor's Manual*. Grand Rapids: Baker, 1973.

Collins, Gary R. *Christian Counseling: A Comprehensive Guide*. Rev. ed. Dallas: Word, 1988.

Curtis, Brent. *Guilt*. Institute for Biblical Counseling Discussion Guide, ed. Tom Varney. Colorado Springs, CO: NavPress, 1992.

Hansel, Tim. *When I Relax I Feel Guilty*. Elgin, IL: David C. Cook, 1979.

Hunt, June. *Counseling Through Your Bible Handbook*. Eugene, Oregon: Harvest House Publishers, 2008.

Hunt, June. *How to Forgive ... When You Don't Feel Like It*. Eugene, Oregon: Harvest House Publishers, 2007.

Hunt, June. *How to Handle Your Emotions*. Eugene, Oregon: Harvest House Publishers, 2008.

Hunt, June. *Seeing Yourself Through God's Eyes*. Eugene, Oregon: Harvest House Publishers, 2008.

Jeffress, Robert. *Guilt-Free Living: How to Know When You've Done Enough*. Wheaton, IL: Tyndale House, 1995.

Johnson, Becca Cowan. *Good Guilt, Bad Guilt: And What to Do with Each*. Downers Grove, IL: InterVarsity, 1996.

Lutzer, Erwin W. *How to Say No to a Stubborn Habit, Even When You Feel Like Saying Yes*. Wheaton, IL: Victor, 1979.

McGee, Robert S. *The Search for Significance:* Book & Workbook. 2nd ed. Houston, TX: Rapha, 1990.

Narramore, Bruce, and Bill Counts. *Freedom from Guilt.* Irvine, CA: Harvest House, 1974.

Parrott, Les, III. *Love's Unseen Enemy: How to Overcome Guilt to Build Healthy Relationships.* Grand Rapids: Zondervan, 1994.

Pentecost, J. Dwight. *Man's Problems—God's Answers.* Chicago: Moody Press, 1971.

Richards, Larry. *Expository Dictionary of Bible Words.* Regency Reference Library. Grand Rapids: Zondervan, 1985.

Splinter, John P. *The Complete Divorce Recovery Handbook.* 2nd ed. Grand Rapids: Zondervan, 1992.

Stanley, Charles F. *Forgiveness.* Nashville: Oliver-Nelson, 1987.

Strong, James. *Strong's Exhaustive Concordance of the Bible.* Nashville: Abingdon, 1986.

June Hunt's HOPE FOR THE HEART minibooks are biblically-based, and full of practical advice that is relevant, spiritually-fulfilling and wholesome.

HOPE FOR THE HEART TITLES

www.aspirepress.com